THE ULTIMATE

Movie Quotes

MOST MEMEORABLE OF ALL TIME

CINEMA FESTIVAL
BEST FILMS

JOURNAL & NOTEBOOK

The Ultimate Guide to Movie Quotes: Most Memorable of all time Journal & Notebook

What is your all-time favorite movie?

"Roads? Where we're going we don't need roads."

Back to the Future, 1985

Have you ever seen the same movie more than once?

"Toto, I've got a feeling we're not in Kansas anymore."

Wizard of OZ, 1933

How often do you go to see movies?

"A million dollars isn't cool. You know what's cool?"

The Social Network, 2010

If a book has been made into a movie, which do you prefer to do first,
see the movie or read the book?

"Carpe diem.
Seize the day, boys.
Make your lives
extraordinary."

Dead Poets Society, 1989

What is the scariest movies you have ever seen?

"Of all the gin joints in all the towns in all the world, she walks into mine."

Casablanca, 1942

What is the worst movie you've ever seen?

"I just wanted to take another look at you."

A Star Is Born, 2018

"Love means never having to say you're sorry."

Love Story, 1970

Who is your favorite actor (female)?

"Say "hello" to my little friend!"

Scarface, 1983

How much money do you spend when you go to movies?

Jamal Malik is one question away from winning 20 million rupees. How did he do it?

A. He cheated
B. He's lucky
C. He's a genius
D. It is written

Slumdog Millionaire, 2008

What is your favorite movie soundtrack?

"Life moves pretty fast.
If you don't stop and look
around once in a while,
you could miss it."

Ferris Bueller's Day Off, 1986

Who is your favorite actor (male)?

"It's good to be the King."

History of the World: Part I, 1981

What do you think about comic books movies?

"Show me the money!"

Jerry Maguire, 1996

Can you remember the name of the first movie you saw that made you cry?

"Soylent Green is people!"

Soylent Green, 1973

Have you ever watched a movie twice that you disliked?

"The first rule of Fight Club is:

You do not talk about Fight Club."

Fight Club, 1999

Have you ever seen a movie in another country? Describe the experience.

"But what I do have are a very particular set of skills, skills I have acquired over a very long career, skills that make me a nightmare for people like you."

Taken, 2008

Do you like foreign films that are dubbed in your mother tongue or do you like watching the film in its original form?

"Why are you wearing that stupid man suit?"

Donnie Darko, 2001

If a movie star wanted to marry you, would you divorce your spouse?

"Nobody, I mean NOBODY puts ketchup on a hot dog."

Sudden Impact, 1983

What is your all-time favorite Christmas movie?

"They call it a Royale with cheese."

Pulp Fiction, 1994

Which famous movie star would you like to have for a best friend?

"Get your stinking paws off me, you damned dirty ape!"

Planet of the Apes, 1968

How often would you go to the movie theater if you always had free tickets?

"Oh, no, it wasn't the airplanes. It was Beauty killed the Beast."

King Kong, 1933

Which horror movie is the scariest you have ever seen? Why?

"Once upon a time, a king gave a feast. And there came the most beautiful princesses of the realm. Now, a soldier, who was standing guard, saw the king's daughter go by. She was the most beautiful one, and he immediately fell in love with her. But what could a poor soldier do when it came to the daughter of the king? Well, finally, one day, he managed to meet her, and he told her that he could no longer live without her. The princess was so impressed by his strong feelings that she said to the soldier: "If you can wait 100 days and 100 nights under my balcony, then at the end of it, I shall be yours." Damn! The soldier immediately went there and waited one day. And two days. And ten. And then twenty. And every evening, the princess looked out of her window, but he never moved. During rain, during wind, during snow, he was always there. The bird shat on his head, and the bees stung him, but he didn't budge. After ninety nights, he had become all dried up, all white, and the tears streamed from his eyes. He couldn't hold them back. He no longer had the strength to sleep. All that time, the princess watched him. And on the 99th night, the soldier stood up, took his chair, and went away."

Cinema Paradiso, 1988

If they made a movie about your life, what kind of movie would it be?

"You're gonna need a bigger boat."

Jaws, 1975

Which actor would be you in a movie about your life?

"My God, it's full of stars."

2001: A Space Odyssey, 1968

What is your all-time favorite Sci-Fi movie?

"I feel the need - the need for speed!"

Top Gun, 1986

Would you rather have a leading role in a movie, or be given $100,000?

"The funny thing is, on the outside I was an honest man. Straight as an arrow. I had to come to prison to be a crook."

Shawshank Redemption, 1994

Would you be willing to be in a movie in only your underwear?

"I see dead people."

The Sixth Sense, 1999

What's the funniest movie you've ever seen?

"Shaken or stirred?"

"Do I look like I give a damn?"

CASINO ROYALE, 2006

If someone were to make a movie about your life, what would you want included?

"I am gonna kill Bill."

Kill Bill: Vol. 2, 2004

Do you usually eat something while you are watching a film?

"They may take our lives, but they'll never take our freedom!"

Braveheart, 1995

What is the first movie you had ever seen in the theater?

"Help me, Obi-Wan Kenobi. You're my only hope."

Star Wars, 1977

Have you ever fallen asleep in the middle of a movie?

"Chancho, when you are a man, sometimes you wear stretchy pants in your room. Just for fun."

Nacho Libre, 2006

Do you choose a film for the plot/story or the actors?

"Yippie-ki-yay, mother—er!"

Die Hard, 1988

What is the longest film you've ever seen?

"I'm king of the world!"

Titanic, 1997

Do you ever go to see movies alone?

"We need Kate, and we need Leo. And we need them now."

Love Actually, 2003

Do you like animated films?

"What makes you think you can just walk in there and find, uh, what we need?"

"They're called boobs, Ed."

Erin Brockovich, 2000

What kind of movie would you like to star in? Why?

"What? Over? Did you say 'over'? Nothing is over until we decide it is! Was it over when the Germans bombed Pearl Harbor? Hell no!.......

Animal House, 1978

What is your all-time favorite romance movie?

"We elves try to stick to the four main food groups: candy, candy canes, candy corns, and syrup."

ELF, 2003

What is your all-time favorite sci-fi movie?

"Scotty, beam me up!"

(not "Beam me up, Scotty!")

Star Trek IV: The Voyage Home, 1986

What is your all-time favorite horror movie?

"Can I borrow your underpants for ten minutes?"

Sixteen Candles, 1984

What is your all-time favorite movie genre?

"Don't you do it! Don't...you... I got nowhere else to go! I got nowhere else to go! I ain't got nothin' else."

An Officer and a Gentleman, 1982

Top 10 Favorite Movies?

"In the face of overwhelming odds, I'm left with only one option. I'm gonna have to science the s--t outta this."

The Martian, 2015

Top 10 Favorite Directors?

"I'm gonna steal the Declaration of Independence."

National Treasure, 2004

Top 10 Favorite Actors (Male)?

"*Hasta la vista*, baby."

Terminator 2: Judgment Day, 1991

Top 10 Favorite Actors (Female)?

"If I'm not back in five minutes, just wait longer."

Ace Ventura: Pet Detective, 1994

Top 10 Favorite Science Fiction?

"To me being a gangster was better than being President of the United States."

GoodFellas, 1990

Top 10 Favorite Foreign Movies?

"Nobody puts Baby in a corner."

Dirty Dancing, 1987

Top 10 Favorite Action Movies?

"I love the smell of napalm in the morning."

Apocalypse Now, 1979

Top 10 Favorite Drama Movies?

"I like them French fried potaters.
Uh-hum."

Sling Blade, 1996

"Well, what if there is no tomorrow?

There wasn't one today."

Groundhog Day, 1993

"Mike. I'm tellin' ya, you're money. You're so f--kin' money!"

Swingers, 1996

So first I go get the money.

Then I go ask Monica.

 say "Monica, you ever been to Mexico, honey?"

I say "Monica, darlin', you coming to Mexico with me?"

"Monica, you coming to Mexico with me!" Me and Monica!

Cos I'm gonna tell you how it's gonna be! Mon-Monica and me! Me and Monica!

Yeah, me and Monica go to Méjico!

Breathless, 1983

BREATHLESS!

Top 10 Favorite Horror Movies?

"Every now and then say, "What the f--k." "What the f--k" gives you freedom. Freedom brings opportunity. Opportunity makes your future."

Risky Business, 1983

"I'll be back."

The Terminator, 1984

**Be excellent to each other.
And PARTY ON, DUDES!"**

Bill & Ted's Excellent Adventure, 1989

Harold: I want 30 sliders, 5 french fries, and 4 large cherry cokes.

Kumar: I want the same except make mine diet cokes.

Harold and Kumar go to White Castle, 2004

"May the Force be with you."

Star Wars, 1977

I Am
the Protagonist.

Tenet, 2020

"To infinity and beyond!"

Toy Story, 1995

"I am Groot."

Guardians of the Galaxy 2014

"Mama always said life was like a box of chocolates. You never know what you're gonna get."

Forrest Gump, 1994

"If my calculations are correct, when this baby hits 88 miles per hour... you're gonna see some serious s--t."

Back to the Future, 1985

If you enjoy this book please leave an Amazon Review.
Let us know some of your favorite movies and quotes.

Made in the USA
Coppell, TX
02 October 2024

38006467R10069